FAMILY LIFE IN
Roman
Britain

PETER CHRISP

Wayland

FAMILY LIFE
SERIES:

Medieval Britain

Roman Britain

Saxon Britain

Second World War

Tudors & Stuarts

Victorian Britain

Series design: Pardoe Blacker Ltd
Editor: Sarah Doughty
Production controller: Carol Stevens

First published in 1994 by Wayland (Publishers) Ltd
61 Western Road, Hove, East Sussex BN3 1JD, England

© Copyright 1994 Wayland (Publishers) Ltd

British Library Cataloguing in Publication Data
Family Life in Roman Britain – (Family Life Series)
  I.Title II.Series
  306.8509361

ISBN 0 7502 1005 2

Printed and bound by Rotolito Lombarda S.p.A.

Cover pictures: (Left) The family god, called a Lar.
(Top) A betrothal ring. (Middle) The hypocaust at Chedworth
Roman villa. (Artwork) A family in a Roman villa.

Picture acknowledgements: Ancient Art & Architecture Collection
8 (right), 10 (top), 12 (top), 14 (both), 17, 25 (right), 28 (bottom);
Audio-Visual Centre 21 (top), 25 (top); Bath Archaeological Trust
12 (bottom), 26 (bottom); City Museum and Art Gallery, Carlisle
11; Colchester Museums 15 (right) 28 (top); County Council and
Bignor Villa 19 (top); English Heritage 23 (top), 27 (bottom); Hull
City Museums and Art Galleries 29 (top); Museum of Antiquities of
the University & Society of Antiquities of Newcastle upon Tyne 7
(right); Museum of London 13 (top), 21 (bottom); The National
Museum of Wales 29 (bottom); National Trust 19 and *cover*;
Reading Museum and Art Gallery 23 (bottom); St Albans Museums
20; Trustees of the British Museum 10 (bottom and cover), 16, 22
and *cover*, 27 (top); Yorkshire Museum 7 (left), 8 (left), 15 (left). All
artwork is by Peter Dennis except 6 (Jenny Hughes).

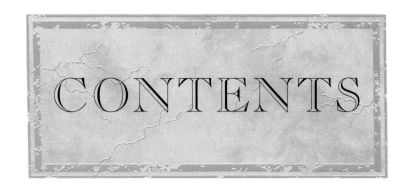

CONTENTS

ROMAN BRITAIN

HADRIAN'S WALL

ALDBOROUGH

YORK

CHESTER

LINCOLN

WROXETER

LEICESTER

GLOUCESTER

COLCHESTER

ST. ALBANS

CIRENCESTER

BATH

LONDON

SILCHESTER

—— MAJOR ROADS

Two thousand years ago, Britain was the home of many different tribes, ruled by kings and queens. The people, called Celts or Britons, spoke a Celtic language which was like Welsh. They lived in small homesteads in round wooden houses. There were no real towns or roads.

Everything changed in the year AD 43, when much of the country was conquered by the Romans. The Romans built Britain's first towns and proper roads. Soon British people learned to speak the Roman language, Latin, as well as Celtic. The wealthier Britons began to dress like Romans and give themselves Roman names. For the first time, Britons learned to read and write. The writer Tacitus described how the Britons were made more like Romans by Agricola, the governor of Britain:

'Agricola helped in the building of temples, public squares and good houses. Furthermore, he gave the sons of the chiefs a Roman education. The result was that, instead of loathing the Latin language they became eager to speak it properly. In the same way, our national dress came into favour and the toga was everywhere to be seen.'

The Romans built dozens of towns throughout Britain, linking them with well-made roads.

The Romans governed Britain for almost four hundred years. Roman rule made British people feel part of a much larger world. The centre of this bigger world was distant Rome. This gave Roman settlers as well as Britons the feeling that they were far away from the centre of things. Gildas, a Roman Briton, wrote:

'The island of Britain lies virtually at the end of the world'.

Before the Romans came, British people lived in tiny homesteads scattered throughout the countryside.

Compare this bustling street from a Roman town with the small homestead. Where would you prefer to live?

THE PEOPLE OF ROMAN BRITAIN

Under Roman rule, people from many other countries came to live in Britain. Roman soldiers from Greece, France, Spain, North Africa, Italy and Syria, settled down and married local women. Women, from Germany and other parts of Northern Europe, also came to Britain, as slaves. The women who were freed from slavery married local people. What held all these different people together was the Roman way of life – the Latin language, the Roman gods and the Roman way of dressing.

Tombstones tell us a lot about the sort of people who lived in Roman Britain. Look at the tombstone on the opposite page, from South Shields in the north of England. It was set up for

*The Roman **Empire** at its greatest size, in the year AD 117. The areas coloured yellow show the Empire.*

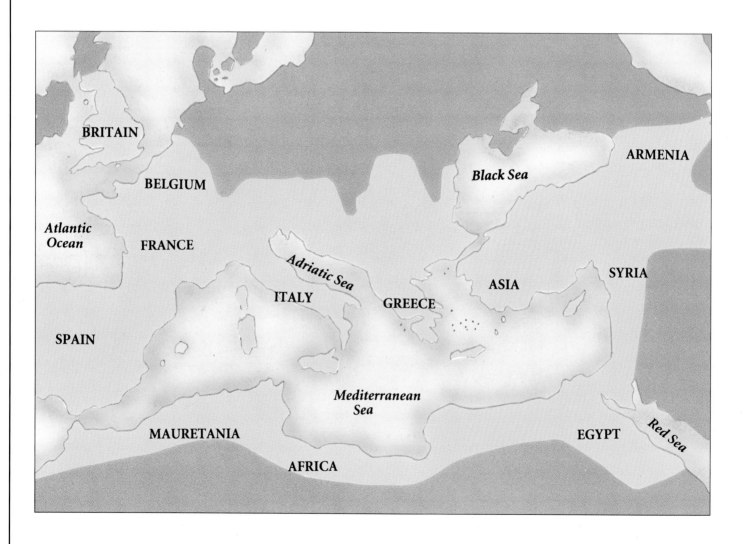

6

a British woman called Regina, by her husband, a man called Barates. He is thought to have been either a soldier or a merchant from Palmyra in Syria, which is a hot country – he must have found his new home very cold and wet. The writing is in Latin and in the language of Palmyra. This shows that, between them, this married couple spoke three languages – Celtic, Latin and Palmyrene.

RICH AND POOR

There were big differences between the lives of rich and poor Roman Britons. The richest gained most from Roman rule. They lived in comfortable houses and buy new luxury goods from overseas. Craftspeople also gained from Roman rule – they set up shops in the new towns.

People who were poor were less affected. They had been poor farmers before the Romans came and they stayed poor farmers. They carried on living in their old wooden homesteads, scattered throughout the countryside.

The tombstone of a British woman who dressed like a Roman and took a Roman name Regina which means 'queen' in Latin. She married Barates from Palmyra in Syria.

(Left) A carving of a smith, hammering a piece of metal into shape, on a York tombstone. The fact that smiths could afford carved tombstones shows how well they prospered under Roman rule.

7

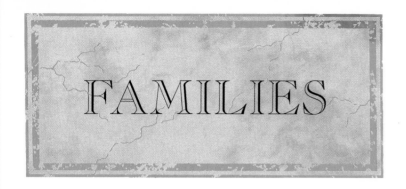

FAMILIES

Roman rule brought big changes to family life in Britain. Before the Romans came, people lived in big extended families. This means that parents, cousins, aunts and uncles all lived in the same small homesteads, helping each other with the farm work and caring for the children. Women were important – we know that some ruled their people as queens.

The Romans had very different ideas about family life and the place and role of women. Instead of living in big extended families, they lived in small family groups where women looked after the home.

Tombstones often show family groups in their homes. This tombstone of Julia Velva from York shows her on a couch, surrounded by her family. She is drinking from a cup and there is food on a table around her.

Upper-class Romans were very proud of their family backgrounds, and they kept the busts of their father and grandfathers in their houses. In time, Roman Britons also began to keep portrait busts.

MEN

In Roman families, men were more valued than women. Sons would bring wealth to a family whereas daughters cost money. They had to be provided with a **dowry** (a sum of money) when they married. Every family was headed by the oldest man, known as the Pater Familias (father of the family). He had the power of life or death over all the family members which included his wife, children, grandchildren and slaves. It was unheard of for men to kill their wives, but they still expected them to stay 'in their place'. Husbands could also divorce their wives if their marriage did not give them any children. The Emperor Augustus made a speech about family life. According to a writer called Cassius Dio, this is how he described the perfect wife:

'What can be better than a wife who stays at home, manages the house for you and brings up your children; who gives you joy when you are well and comfort when you are sick; who shares your successes and consoles you for your failures.'

How do you think a Roman wife might feel about this description of her role? Roman Britain was a country run by men. Only men could follow public careers in politics or law. Men could be **citizens** – people with full rights, which included voting in elections. Women were not allowed to do these things. Occasionally women complained about their lack of **equality**.

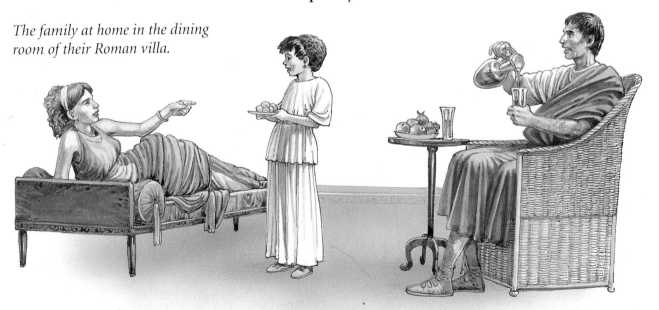

The family at home in the dining room of their Roman villa.

MARRIAGE

Husbands were usually much older than their wives. This was especially true of Romans who came to Britain as soldiers. They were expected to wait until they gave up soldiering, in their 40s, before they settled down with a wife. Women were usually married between the ages of 18 and 28.

The marriage was usually arranged by the groom or his father and the father of the bride. There was often a **betrothal** ceremony, where the groom gave the bride a ring. This was worn on the finger on which people today still wear wedding rings. A writer called Aulus Gellius suggested why this finger was chosen:

'When the human body is cut open, a very delicate nerve is found which starts from this finger and travels to the heart.'

The wedding ceremony usually took place at the house of the bride. Here the couple promised in front of witnesses to live as husband and wife. The aim of the marriage was to have children, especially boys. If the couple was divorced, the man had to return the dowry.

This carving, from Italy, shows a wedding ceremony. The bride and groom clasp hands, as a mark of their agreement. In his other hand, the groom holds the marriage contract.

The giving of rings is one wedding custom that can be traced back to the Romans. On one of these rings you can see clasped hands again.

WOMEN

Rich Roman men expected their wives to look after the house and to care for the children. For the women, this meant giving orders to the household slaves: sending them out to do the shopping and telling them what to cook for dinner.

Look back at the carving of Regina, on page 7. On one side she has a strong box, for the family valuables – this shows her role in running the household. On her other side, she has a basket holding balls of wool. Women like Regina spent a lot of time spinning wool into thread using a piece of wood or bone, called a spindle, weighted with a small piece of stone or bone called a whorl. Many of these have been found in Roman sites. The writing on women's tombstones tells us what men expected of them. The writings often say,

'She stayed at home, she worked at her wool.'

Only the better-off Roman Britons could afford for their wives to stay at home and run the household. Poorer women would have to work alongside their husbands, in the shop or out in the fields.

A rich woman fans herself while watching her child play with a pet bird in her lap. This carving, from Carlisle, gives a good idea of the clothes worn by wealthy women.

This coin shows the young Emperor Nero with his mother, Agrippina. Coins like this could show Roman Britons the latest fashions in hairstyles in far off Rome.

FASHION

Rich women were very interested in fashion and hairstyles were often changing. New styles came from Rome, especially from the family of the **Emperor**. Although there were no fashion magazines for keeping in touch with Roman styles, there were coins which carried portraits of the **Empress**. British women could see the latest hairstyles by looking at their coins. Some of their hairstyles were very elaborate, as you can see from the carving below. This woman has tight curls, arranged in rows piled on top of each other. This might have been done with heated curling tongs, but it is just as likely to be a wig.

Men's hairstyles also changed. As with women, the lead came from the ruling family. For example, the Emperor Nero is shown on this coin with short hair. Later on, he grew his hair until it reached his shoulders, and men all over the Empire copied him. Another Emperor, **Hadrian**, made beards popular.

It was fashionable for women to wear perfume and make-up. They blackened their eyebrows with a mixture of soot and bear fat and reddened their cheeks and lips with red wine dregs.

Women's hairstyles were at their most elaborate between AD 80 and 100, when this carving from Bath was made. Do you think this shows real hair or a wig?

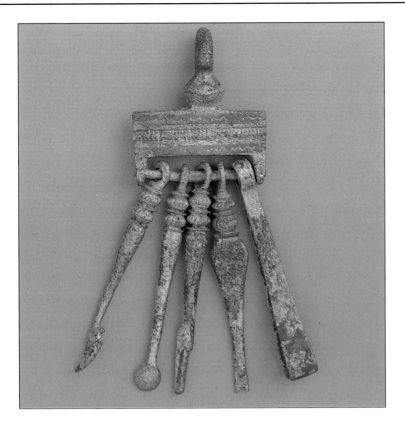

This manicure set once dangled from a woman's belt. It includes a round scoop for make-up, a nail file, a pointed tool for cleaning the nails and tweezers (used by men and women for plucking out their body hair).

CLOTHES

Before the Roman conquest, British men wore ankle-length trousers. Under the Romans, they stopped wearing trousers and began to wear a knee-length tunic over bare legs. For important occasions, men who were Roman citizens wore a toga, a large white woollen sheet, wrapped in complicated folds. Women wore a longer tunic, covered by a gown. Both men and women wore cloaks to keep warm. These could be short, fastened at the shoulder by a brooch, or they might be long and heavy with a hood. Rich people could afford colourful clothes made from linen and silk. Poorer people dressed simply, wearing plain coloured rough wool.

(Below) This shows the typical clothes worn by Roman Britons. The man wears a short tunic covered with a cloak. The woman wears a longer tunic covered by a garment called a palla. Like the toga, this was made from a piece of rectangular material.

CHILDREN

Children were usually born at home, helped by a midwife. Birth was very risky in Roman times because nobody realized that dirt carried germs. As a result, mothers and their new babies often fell ill. One Roman **cemetery**, at Poundbury in Dorset, held the graves of 281 women. Fifty-one of them had died as a result of giving birth. Many children also died young, because of all the diseases for which there were not yet cures.

LESSONS

Only the children of wealthy people had any formal education. Boys and girls were taught reading and writing by their mothers, or by slaves. They used wooden writing tablets coated with wax. They practised making letters by scratching them on the wax with a pointed piece of metal.

In the schools, the sons of the richer Roman Britons learned how to speak in public. This was an important skill for anyone who wanted a career in law or politics. Rich girls learned different skills at home – music, dancing, spinning and weaving.

Poorer children would have had hardly any education. They were expected to help their parents with their work (for example, farming) from a very young age.

Children practised writing on wax tablets using a pointed piece of metal called a stylus. The wax tablet is a modern copy.

For craftsmen, like this blacksmith, working life and family life were the same thing. You can see the blacksmith's children helping him with his work. There are also other details of the home – loaves of bread on the table and a pet dog.

CHILDREN'S GAMES

Children played with wood or rag dolls, and with toy animals and carts. Some Roman toys have survived and we know more about them thanks to descriptions in Roman books. Children also played lots of different games, including leap frog and ball games. One ball game was called trigon. This needed three players and three balls. The players stood in a triangle, each throwing the ball to the person on their right, at the same time catching the ball thrown by the person on their left.

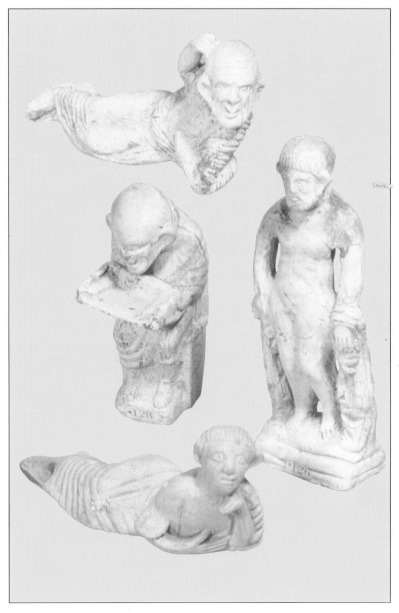

(Above) Tombstones showed that children dressed just like their parents. On this tombstone from York, the whole family is dressed in thick coats and ankle boots. The two children are holding balls to play with. They both died before they were 2 years old.

(Right) Children's toys are sometimes found in their graves, like these figures found in Colchester. The two figures lying down are diners, relaxing after a meal. The man holding what looks like a tray is entertaining the others by reading a story.

SLAVES

The Romans, like almost all ancient peoples, kept slaves and rich Roman Britons did as well. Slaves were people who were bought and sold and treated as property. They might be captured in war; they might be the children of slave parents; or they might be sold into slavery by their parents.

No Roman thought that there was anything wrong with slavery, though some said that slaves should be kindly treated. A writer called Seneca wrote to a friend:

'I am glad to hear that you are on friendly terms with your slaves. They may be slaves but they are also men – men with whom we share the same roof, our humble friends.'

Small bronze jars, shaped like sleeping boy slaves were popular ornaments. Perhaps the Romans felt sorry for they boys, tired out after long hours of work; or perhaps they thought the slaves were lazy. What do you think?

Wealthy Romans had slaves to do almost everything for them. Here you can see two slaves working on their mistress's hair while a third holds a mirror. Imagine having three people to help you dress each morning!

Slaves who pleased their owners by working well could earn their freedom. If you look again at the carving of Regina, on page 7, you'll see the world 'LIBERTA' ('freedwoman'). This means that Regina had once been a slave but had been freed by her owner. As a freedwoman, Regina would have slaves of her own.

Women slaves helped the mistress dress each morning; they prepared and served the meals; and they nursed their owners' children with their own milk. Male slaves had to carry their owners through the streets on a litter (a small carriage on poles). If they were educated, they might act as teachers for the children. A rich Roman couldn't have imagined life without slaves.

AT HOME

In the towns, ordinary people lived in simple houses with wooden frames and walls made of 'wattle' (twigs) and 'daub' (clay). The houses of craftspeople and traders were often long and narrow. One end faced the street and served as a shop front.

Wealthier people could afford much grander homes. These were often rectangular, with rooms ranged around a courtyard, planted as a garden. The windows would be mostly on the inside walls facing the garden. This kept out the noise of the street and made the house more private.

The rich loved to decorate their homes with colourful wall paintings and floor mosaics – pictures made from hundreds of tiny coloured tiles. Mosaics were used to show complicated patterns, animals, fish plants and scenes from Roman stories.

Rich Roman Britons lived in houses like this. The living quarters are on two floors, with windows facing the garden courtyard.

A mosaic of the goddess, Venus, from Bignor in Sussex. Think how long it took to make this picture out of tiny tiles! Only the richest Roman Britons could afford mosaics like this, and they only had them in the most important rooms of the house.

CENTRAL HEATING

Many Roman settlers in Britain came from the warm lands of the south. To them, Britain was a cold place. The Romans found a way of warming up their houses using a type of central heating called a **hypocaust**. This used a furnace where charcoal was burned. The hot air was then channelled through gaps under the floors, which were raised on brick columns.

Remains of hypocausts have been found in several villas, grand country farmhouses which belonged to wealthy Roman Britons. Some villas also had their own private bath houses, with rooms for hot, cold and steam baths.

This is the hypocaust (under-floor heating) in baths at Chedworth Roman villa. The floor was raised on the pillars of tiles which you can see in the foreground. The hot air passed through the gaps between the pillars.

FOOD AND COOKING

We know the sort of food that Roman Britons ate, thanks to the food remains found in their rubbish pits. Bones, shells, fruit pips and charred grains can all help to build up a picture of meals in Roman Britain. By discovering bird bones, for example, we know that people ate the meat of swans, thrushes, jackdaws, crows, herring gulls and storks. Fish was also very popular, especially shellfish such as oysters. Oyster shells have been found in almost all the Roman rubbish pits in Britain, no matter how far from the sea.

Before the Romans came to Britain, British people drank beer made from barley. Poorer people still continued to drink this, but richer Roman Britons preferred wine. Some wine was made from grapes grown in the south of England, but most was brought from France in pottery jars called amphoras. Another important product from abroad was olive oil, used

These Roman pots and bowls were found in St Albans. You can also see some of the things that the people of St Albans ate. Grapes, which could only be grown in the south of England, were one of the many new foods bought by the Romans.

Wine was served in different ways. Sometimes it was heated by pouring it over hot coals held in a colander – the object in the centre of this picture. It could also be cooled by being poured over ice.

in cooking and oil lamps. Most of the olive oil came from Spain. The Romans introduced many new herbs and spices to Britain, including mustard, mint, coriander and dill. They also loved the spicy, salty taste of garum, a sauce made from the guts of fish. Like we use tomato ketchup today, people put garum on lots of different things. Another popular flavour was honey, used instead of sugar. Fish sauce and honey are found in many Roman recipes, often together in the same dish.

People ate their main meal in the late afternoon or early evening. They ate lying down on couches, picking at the dishes with their fingers. There were knives, but no forks in Roman times.

This reconstruction at the Museum of London shows what a Roman kitchen looked like. On the right you can see the raised hearth. Charcoal was burned on top, heating the pot on the gridiron. The long clay amphoras (storage jars) held oil, wine, vinegar and fish sauce.

HOUSEHOLD GODS

The Romans believed that every house had its own gods, taking care of everyone who lived there. The Penates were gods who protected the larder, making sure that food supplies weren't eaten by mice. There was also a god called the family **Lar**, who watched over all the family members.

People kept little metal statues of these gods in their houses. In rich houses, they were kept in a special **shrine**, which was like a small **temple**. Poorer people kept cheaper statues of family gods on a simple wooden shelf. Each day, the women of the house would take flowers and small offerings of food to the gods. This was thought to bring good luck.

This tiny figure is a family Lar, a god who watched over every house and family. He is usually shown as a young dancing man, holding a dish and a wine jug.

Roman Britons loved playing board games and gambling with dice. Here you can see some gaming pieces, a board, some dice and the cups used for shaking them.

A family Lar appears as a character in a Roman play, by Plautus. This is how he introduces himself:

'I am the family Lar, the guardian spirit of this house. I have been in charge of this house now for a great many years. I have watched over it for the present owner, and his father, and his grandfather.'

GAMES AND MUSIC

Roman Britons had lots of different ways of having fun at home. They relaxed by gambling with dice and playing board games. The board game you can see here was called 'soldiers'. It was a bit like draughts, except the aim was to capture enemy pieces by surrounding them.

Another way of relaxing was with music and dancing. Women in particular were often skilled musicians, playing stringed instruments, such as lyres, and pipes. They would entertain the rest of the family after dinner. Unfortunately, we have no way of knowing what the music sounded like.

This statue shows a young woman holding a musical instrument called a 'tibia' – a pipe, like a flute, made from a hollow reed.

TOWN LIFE

The Romans believed that civilized living meant town life. A Roman town was the centre of local government. It was also a market place, for buying and selling goods from abroad as well as things made locally. It was a place for relaxing too, with theatres and public baths. The centre of each town was the forum, which was both a market place and the site of the basilica, a large hall where the town council met and where law cases were heard.

Towns looked much the same throughout the Roman Empire. There was always a big square forum, surrounded by temples and bath houses.

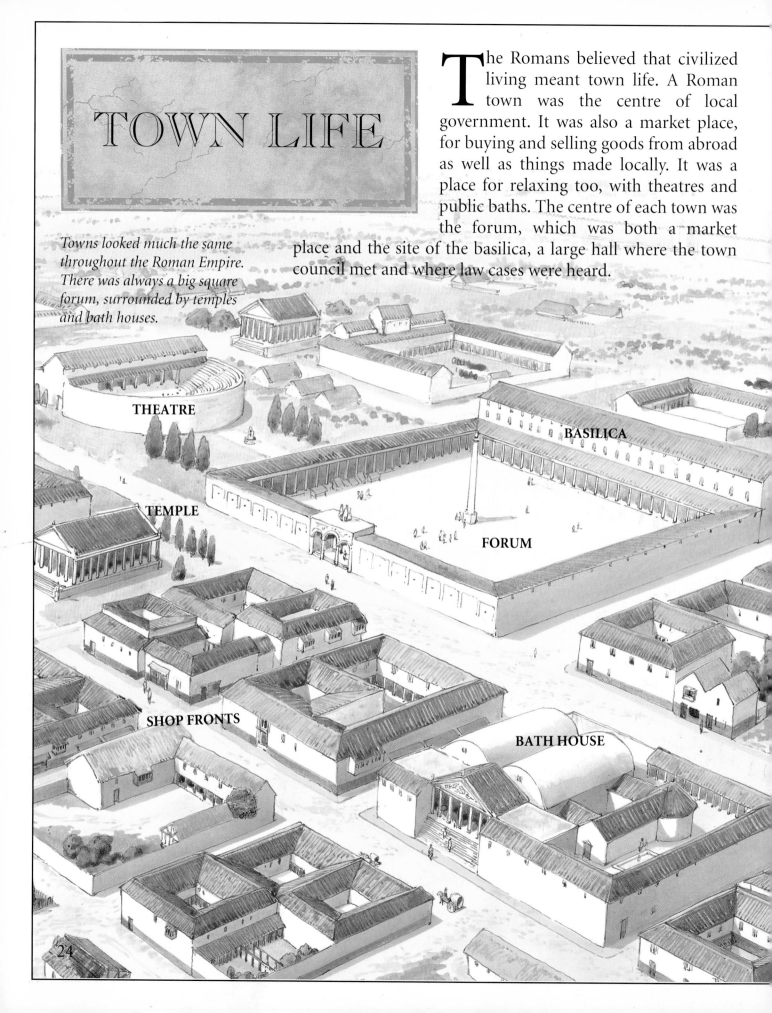

THEATRE

BASILICA

TEMPLE

FORUM

SHOP FRONTS

BATH HOUSE

TEMPLES

Towns were also religious centres, with temples dedicated to the most important Roman gods. For example, there was Jupiter, king of the gods, and his wife Juno, goddess of mothers. Some of the Roman gods became mixed up with old British gods – Sulis Minerva, a healing goddess who had a temple at Bath, was a mixture of the Roman goddess, Minerva, and the British goddess, Sulis.

This is all that remains of a temple of the god, Mithras, from Carrawburgh in Northumberland. Mithras, mainly worshipped by Roman soldiers and merchants, originally came from Iran.

Religion was the one place outside the home where women could play an important role. This is a priestess, getting ready to make an offering to a god.

Each temple had a large statue of the god who was worshipped there. There was also a staff of priests and priestesses to serve the god. Ordinary people went to the temple to offer a gift to the god, hoping for a favour in return. We know what sort of favours they asked because they wrote them down on pieces of lead. For example, a Norfolk man wrote to the god Neptune to tell him that he had had some money and other valuables stolen from him. He asked the god to kill the thief, promising to give Neptune a new pair of leggings in return.

HOT

VERY WARM

WARM

COLD

FURNACE HYPOCAUST

Each bath house had a series of rooms which were kept at different temperatures. This cutaway diagram shows how this was done. The hottest rooms were those nearest the furnace.

A VISIT TO THE BATHS

One of the most important buildings in every town was the bath house. This was a place where people would go every day to bathe, exercise, relax and meet friends. Public baths included a courtyard for exercise and a series of rooms, heated to different temperatures. There was a hot steamy room where you could sit and sweat; a warm room where you could lie and soak; and a cold room where you could have a quick refreshing plunge.

Like central heating in Roman villas, the water and the rooms of the bath house were heated by furnaces. Slaves had to keep these furnaces stoked with wood. Other slaves carried towels and gave massages to the bathers. The Romans had not invented soap. Instead they rubbed their bodies with olive oil, brought from overseas, and then scraped the oil and dirt off with a curved bronze tool called a strigil.

The Roman baths at Bath used naturally hot water, from a spring. People believed that this hot water could cure many different illnesses. They came from all over the Roman Empire to try it.

The public baths needed huge amounts of running water, brought in pipes from local springs and rivers. This water was also needed to flush the toilets, also found in bath houses. There were no private cubicles in the toilets – going to the toilet was a social activity and people sat together in rows. Instead of toilet paper, they used sea sponges on sticks. Tiny fragments of these sponges have been found in Roman sewers.

Think what it must have been like for a Briton visiting a bath house for the first time. Before the Romans came, there were no such places. Those first Britons must have been amazed by them.

A visitor to the baths would take along a jar of oil, for rubbing into the skin, and a curved strigil, for scraping off the oil and dirt.

Twenty men at a time could use this toilet, from the Roman fort at Housesteads. They sat on wooden seats around the edge.

ENTERTAINMENT

Towns were also popular places for public entertainment. Some of the major towns, such as Colchester, Canterbury and St Albans, had theatres where plays were put on with music and dancing. The actors wore masks, showing the sort of characters they were playing and the type of play they were in. Grinning masks were for a comedy; sad or frowning masks, like the one on the next page, were for **tragedy**.

More popular than the theatre was the amphitheatre – a big round space where people could watch fights between gladiators. Gladiators were slaves or criminals who were forced to fight to the death for the entertainment of others. They also fought wild

(Above) This vase from Colchester shows a fight between two gladiators. This may be a fight that really took place since the fighters' names – Memnon and Valentinus – are written above them. Valentinus has just lost. He has dropped his weapons and is holding up his finger to ask for mercy.

(Below) At St Albans, you can still make out the shape of the ancient Roman theatre. It was used both for plays and religious festivals in honour of the gods.

28

The horses gallop around the track in a mosaic of a chariot race, from Horkstow in Lincolnshire.

animals, especially bears, which still roamed Scotland in those days. Scottish bears were sent all the way to Rome to fight in the amphitheatre.

Roman Britons also loved watching chariot races. Teams of horses pulled their chariots at great speed around a large oblong track. There were different chariot companies known by different colours – red, green, white and blue. Just like football teams today, each colour had its own supporters. People gambled on their favourite team.

The mosaic at the top of the page shows how dangerous a sport chariot racing could be. Look at the chariot at the top left which has just reached the turning on the track.

Can you see the wheel that has just come flying off? The two horsemen at the top are dashing to the rescue.

We know what the masks worn by actors looked like thanks to carvings of them, which people had as decorations in their homes. The masks themselves have not lasted because they were made of wood.

GLOSSARY

Betrothal An engagement to be married.

Cemetery A place where dead people are buried.

Citizen A member of a state. Someone who has rights, such as the right to vote, in that state.

Civilized A society that is highly-ordered. For example, one with law and order, education and practical comforts.

Dowry Money or property given by a woman's family to her husband at marriage.

Emperor The man who held supreme power in the Empire.

Empire A large area, including more than one country, controlled by a single state.

Empress The wife of an Emperor.

Equality Being equal. All people having the same rights and opportunities.

Furnace A structure like an oven, that produced great heat.

Hadrian The Emperor who is famous for building a wall across Britain.

Hypocaust Space under a floor heated by air from a furnace; a form of central heating.

Lar A god thought to protect a Roman house.

Shrine Anything containing something holy. Roman houses had 'household shrines', where small statues of gods were kept.

Temple A building made for the worship of a god.

Toga A large woollen sheet worn in a complicated system of folds by Roman men.

Tragedy A serious play with an unhappy ending, showing the sufferings of a hero or heroine.

BOOKS TO READ

Marsden, Barry, *Roman Invaders and Settlers* (Wayland, 1992)

Osband, Gillian, *Roman Britain* (Kingfisher Books, National Trust, 1989)

Renfrew, Jane, *Food and Cooking in Roman Britain* (English Heritage, 1989)

Hall, Jenny and Jones, Christine, *Roman Britain* (BBC Educational Publishing, 1992)

O'Connell, Martin, *Roman Britain* (Wayland, 1989)

Corbishley, Mike, *Everyday Life in Roman Times* (Watts Books, 1993)

James, Simon, *Ancient Rome* (Dorling Kindersley Eyewitness Guides, 1991)

PLACES TO VISIT

Arbeia Roman Fort, Baring Street, South Shields, Tyne and Wear.
This is one of the forts of Hadrian's Wall. The museum has some of the best Roman British carved tombstones, including that of Regina, shown on page 7.

Bath Roman Museum, Abbey Churchyard, Bath, Avon.
This includes the famous Roman baths.

Bignor Roman Villa, near Arundel, West Sussex.
This has beautiful mosaics, such as the picture of Venus on page 19.

Corinium Museum, Park Street, Cirencester, Gloucestershire.
This museum has Roman sculpture, mosaics and reconstructions of kitchen and a dining room.

Fishbourne Roman Palace, Salthill Road, near Chichester, West Sussex.
Thought to be the great palace of the British king Cogidubnus. Fine mosaics and a replanted Roman garden.

Verulamium Museum, St Albans, Hertfordshire.
Finds from the third largest Roman city in Britain. Nearby, you can visit a Roman theatre.

INDEX